# Philadelphia's MAGIC GARDENS

Text by Betsy Augustine
Photographs by Barry Halkin

## THE ART OF ISAIAH ZAGAR

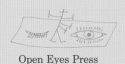

Open Eyes Press

"I read a short story, I don't remember when (long ago), I see it as a movie. I close my eyes. An old man, he wears a dark suit, he walks slowly with the aid of a cane. He walks from an open road to a town. As he passes each house in the town he scans it, his eyes very bright. He is counting bricks! He was a mason in his working life. I see him finally leaving the town; nobody knows him there. The road opens. His back is to me. He set all the bricks in all the buildings of the town!"

—Isaiah

Preceding page:
"Eddie Mattio is
the 3rd genera-
tion plumber, his
son works with
him, a 4th gener-
ation plumber.
Eddie wanted to
celebrate his fa-
ther Mike. He
commisioned me
to make a Mosaic.
I asked Eddie for
a photograph. He
presented me
with a photograph
I had taken 20
years ago of his
father. I made
Mike's face in
tiles with the aid
of that photo-
graph."

Isaiah on his
rooftop of 1003
Kater Street
studio.

"Hello, Benny, hello Abie"

When you recover from the shock of seeing an entire building in downtown Philadelphia covered with tiny bits of mirror and broken tile, your feelings change to either delight and curiosity or to dismay and horror. In any case you'll probably wonder "What's going on here?"

The answer involves Isaiah and Julia Zagar, artists and urban pioneers who moved into the half-deserted area of Philadelphia known as lower South Street in 1968, having just completed a 3 year stint with the Peace Corps working as Art Advisors to the Aymara and Inca people of the Andes mountains of Perú. Isaiah was born in 1939 and grew up in Brooklyn, NY, receiving his B.A. from Pratt Institute in Brooklyn in 1960. Isaiah majored in Graphics and Painting. Julia grew up in Manhattan and graduated from Cooper Union, after which she spent a year studying painting in Mexico City at the University of the Americas. They met and married in 1962. Julia's interest in the Latin American culture has continued through the years. For 31 years she has run the Eyes Gallery at 402 South Street, their family business which sells folk art, clothing, jewelry, and furniture from all over the world. Julia brings Latin American artisans/artists to Philadelphia

Interior of the Eyes Gallery, with Latin American Folk Art. Notice mosaic on right depicting Julia and Isaiah Zagar

to demonstrate their crafts at schools and colleges and promote cultural exchange with Mexico and Latin America.

Beginning in 1979 Isaiah has received sporadic recognition from mainstream art establishments in Philadelphia and nationally. In that year he was given both a $10,000 NEA Fellowship grant and a solo exhibition of his work at the Morris Gallery of the Pennsylvania Academy of Fine Arts in Philadelphia. In 1995 The Philadelphia Print Center exhibited 150 of his autobiographical narrative etchings, and in 1996 The Pew Foundation awarded him a $50,000 Artist Grant. Yet despite this level of art education and sophistication, Isaiah calls himself a "Folk" artist. Roger Manley and Mark Sloan in their '97 Aperture Press book, *Self-Made Worlds-Visionary Folk Art Environments* agree with this self-definition. They include Isaiah's Philadelphia street mosaics in their Global List of Visionary Folk Art Environment Sites.

While still a student at Pratt, a friend took Isaiah to Woodstock, New York, to see the environment Clarence Schmidt built over a period of 40 years. Isaiah describes this space as a huge garden full of mirrors, with trees wrapped in aluminum foil. Isaiah has called it the single most important day of his life. However it was 10 years before Isaiah would begin work on his own folk environment. His mosaic work began in 1969 after the nervous breakdown

Mildred Street wall, between 8th and 9th streets. "I didn't know John Geta. He was an old man who watched me working every day on the 'Church of the Crucifixion' wall. 'Hey professor,' he said finally, 'what is your next project?' 'I don't have one' I said. 'Come here' he motioned me to a graffiti-filled wall on Mildred Street opposite his home. John organized the neighbors, 2 days of picnicking and hard work." June 1996.

"I sit in front of the wall with my father every nice morning having coffee."

he suffered while struggling to readjust to life in the USA. His breakdown occurred while he was working on, but had been unable to finish a large painting depicting his three years in Peru. When he recovered from the breakdown he found the rectangular shape of a canvas was too confining. He describes the relief he experienced when he began making mosaics: "...it didn't matter how I terminated the day's work . . . in fact I had no boundaries . . . I just placed one object next to another. I found myself with a sense of such pleasure at having objects stick and melding  them together with color tinted cement . . . Once everything was grouted there was no way that you could remove pieces easily, so I had to be content with what I got. I couldn't 'turn on the judge' and say 'just erase one line, and put in another, all would be perfect.' It is always perfect!"

The folk art objects Julia buys for their store are often broken in transit. Isaiah says they still contain much of their original

Left: John Geta Memorial. Pemberton St. between 8th and 9th streets.

Above: Detail of "Tony's Wall" Pemberton Street between 8th and 9th streets.

13

power of expression, so he saves them to perhaps one day include in a wall. He receives scrap material from many different sources—so much that storage has become a problem. His fondness for including bits of mirror in his murals is related to his dyslexia. He says that the quality of reversal has always interested him and is what attracted him to printmaking, where everything is reversed. He describes dyslexics, as people who are "not tightly metered or very rational, but are all over the place in their concentration." Making mosaics has allowed him "to concentrate on macrocosmos and microcosmos at the same time. I never get tired of working. The mirror is endless energy, reflecting everything." Twenty of Zagar's mosaic street murals can be seen within a 10-12 block area in the South Street section of Philadelphia. Six more murals are in the Old City section. The Painted Bride Art Center at 230 Vine Street, whose five sides are totally embellished in shimmering bits of mirror and tile, is perhaps Zagar's grand opus. The work was done as a gift from the artist to "The Bride"—a community art center Isaiah helped found. In its infancy it was in a

610 South 10th St. backyard embellished in 1990 under extreme pressure. "My first floor tenants were suspected of operating a crack house. I worked and watched. Finally I saw what I needed to and I began eviction proceedings. In the process I embellished every available space, including the fire escape."

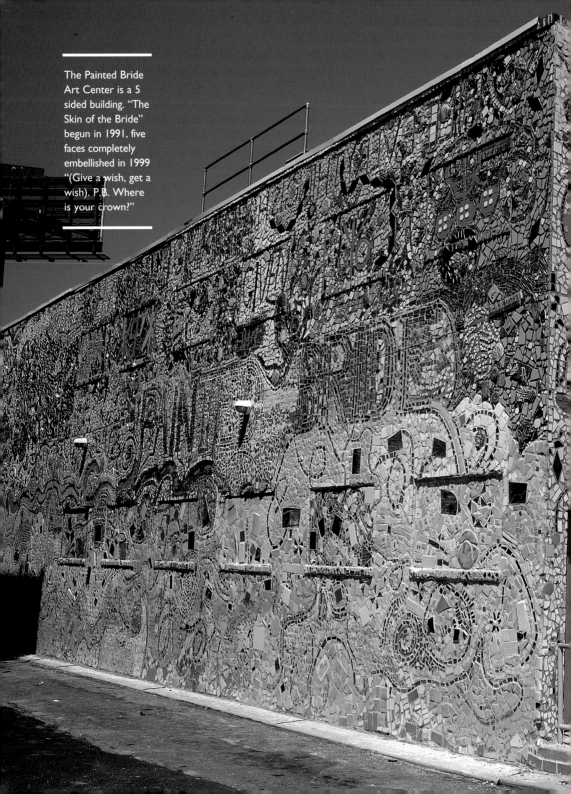

The Painted Bride
Art Center is a 5
sided building. "The
Skin of the Bride"
begun in 1991, five
faces completely
embellished in 1999
"(Give a wish, get a
wish). P.B. Where
is your crown?"

Photograph by Don Camera, 1993

rented space on South Street. There
Isaiah and a group of artists met to
exchange ideas, and show their work.

Isaiah has made most of his street
mosaics at his own expense, preferring
not to concern himself with someone
else's "program."

He says he doesn't know WHY he
makes the murals, only that he feels
he MUST. The idea of making a walk-
ing tour of art occurred to him after a
visit to Florence, Italy. The fact that
strangers enjoy his work satisfies him
that what he is expressing is not sim-
ply personal, but something ap-
preciated by many. He refers to the
process as a sharing of dreams.

Isaiah chooses to build his "poems"
(his designation for his mosaic walls)
in the neighborhood which he says
has made him what he is. The Zagars'

life has been inextricably involved in the growth of that neighborhood. They were among the first young people to move there when, in 1969, the street was a half-boarded-up urban desert. Their Peace Corps training prepared them to take leadership roles in community building. As more people moved into the vacated buildings, the Zagars were busy helping in many ways, particularly in building networks of support for the new area residents. Many of these original residents have moved away but the Zagars remain, adjusting to the ever-changing character of their neighborhood.

While Zagar's first mosaic murals appeared on his own properties, they soon showed up in the alleys behind these properties and from there to nearby side streets. His goal, he says, is to live in an expanding world of his own creation, as Simon Rodia's "our town" in Watts, Los Angeles, Joseph Ferdinand Cheval's "palace of the imagination" in Hauterives, Drôme, France, Antonio Gaudí's Güell Park in Barcelona, Spain, and Nek Chand's "rock garden" in Chandigarh, India.

The reason Isaiah uses so much mirror in his work is to remind each passing observer: "Yes, it's YOU. YOU'RE here. YOUR dreams matter too."

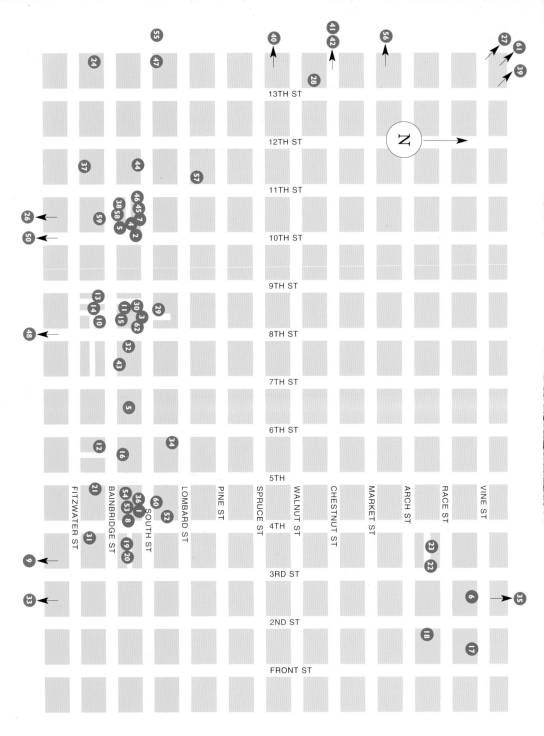

13TH ST

12TH ST

N

11TH ST

10TH ST

9TH ST

8TH ST

7TH ST

6TH ST

5TH

4TH

3RD ST

2ND ST

FRONT ST

FITZWATER ST
BAINBRIDGE ST
SOUTH ST
LOMBARD ST
PINE ST
SPRUCE ST
WALNUT ST
CHESTNUT ST
MARKET ST
ARCH ST
RACE ST
VINE ST

**Isaiah Zagar**   http://www.isaiahzagar.com